7194

THE ART OF STAIR BUILDING,

WITH ORIGINAL IMPROVEMENTS,

DESIGNED TO ENABLE EVERY CARPENTER IN THE COUNTRY TO LEARN THE
BUSINESS IN THE MOST PERFECT MANNER, BY THE EASIEST METHODS.

WITH NUMEROUS ILLUSTRATIONS,

SHOWING AT A GLANCE THE DIFFICULT PARTS OF THE ART, AND MAKING ALL
PLAIN AND COMPREHENSIVE.

BY J. R. PERRY,
Stair Builder.

Published by ~~the Author~~. *A. Ranney*
NEW YORK, 1855. *195 Broadw*

EK

Entered, according to Act of Congress, in the year 1855,
By J. R. PERRY,
in the Clerk's Office of the District Court of the United States, for
the Southern District of New York.

P 4

TIEN & STERNER, Lithographers and Printers, 90 Fulton Street, N. Y.

INTRODUCTION.

From the numerous works already published on the subject of stair building it might seem useless to add another. But feeling from the nature of those now before the public a demand for something more concise and yet complete in itself, containing the latest improvements as well as introducing much which is *entirely new and original,* I offer this to the public.

It has been the practice with most authors on this subject, to treat it in so *professedly* a scientific manner, as almost entirely to obscure it from the ordinary mind with technicalities and unnecessary explanations, thereby defeating the ostensible object of their labors.

It is therefore considered useless to give plans and rules which would be of no purpose, but to exercise the mathematical fancy of the student, who would not be benefited by them in a practical way; and as those methods which require the least consideration and study, and which may be executed in the shortest time, are to be mostly desired by the practical mechanic, such only are given.

The principal consideration in bringing out treatise has been, to make it useful, and consequently no pains have been spared, to make it simple and easy of comprehension. By the straightforward and natural manner adopted in describing the various diagrams, the expeditious mode of executing them, and reducing the number of lines for each to as few as possible, it is hoped this end is attained.

A multiplicity of lines always tends to confuse the mind, and is an objection of the most serious character, and in fact, the principal complaint with workmen generally, is, fixing so many lines on the memory.

Another difficulty seems to be the methods adopted in explaining the diagrams; for instance:

I am told to draw a line from t to u, produce it to c, bisect at o and make b d &c. &c.

But of the *philosophy* of these lines I am not informed. I may be able to lay down the figures, but to comprehend them in a proper manner *from their descriptions* is entirely out of the question.

It requires a thorough mathematical knowledge to understand many of the problems laid down on this subject, and when fully comprehended, they only show the fact, that they are merely scientific in appearance and not in reality, and only demonstrate the absurdity of the premises taken, and the language used to describe them rather conceals, than reveals, their true merit.

The technicalities used to decorate such productions may speak well for their authors in a literary sense, with a certain class; but the practical workman will no doubt appreciate something better adapted to his present wants.

Profiting by a knowledge of these facts, acquired by observations made while teaching my plans in various parts of the county, I have endeavored as much as possible to avoid these difficulties, and to improve this work so, as to make it acceptable to mechanics generally. For this purpose an explanation of terms is introduced, also an entire different style of explaining the plates and diagrams, which give the reasons for making every line. The instructions are gradual and progressive in their character, from the most simple Ideas on, to the more difficult of comprehension, and a continuous chain of thought is preserved throughout, thus making it interesting and instructive without tiring the mind, and it is confidently believed, that if the reasons given in another part of this work are carefully studied and experimentally carried out, they will be adopted by every one, who may have an opportunity of examining them, and soon introduced to make them of great advantage to carpenters. *For*

at least one half the labor ordinarily required in
Spiral hand rails alone, is dispensed with by these
plans.

A great variety of plans are not given, as it
would only enhance the price of the work, without
benefiting the workman, but a sufficient number in
variety are given to impart the principles of stair building, and its modifications are left to the discretion of
the workman, and the circumstances necessarily atten-
ding this business.

In a word, it is offered to the public with a full
impression, that it contains information for the practical stair builder, which has never been published
and many improvements made, on the old plans laid
down by authors long ago, as also the methods of
getting the face mould &c. being entirely new.

Without attempting to detract from the merits of
these authors, it would only be false modesty to refrain
from saying plainly, what is generally insinuated; that
it is offered as an improvement on works of this kind.
And I depend for success in the undertaking, on the
discriminating intelligence of my fellow mechanics.

J. R. PERRY, Architect and Builder,

AN EXPLANATION OF TERMS USED IN STAIR BUILDING.

It might be thought by many to be unnecessary to introduce this in a work of this kind, as the terms are so common and general. But it should be remembered that all who wish to become, are not stair builders, let the following anecdote illustrate.

While giving lessons in Newburg, N. Y., a young man, who wishing to become acquainted with this branch of business, concluded to take lessons, but said, he could not understand the terms and feared some trouble in this respect, whereupon I agreed to make all plain. In the course of the lesson I frequently made use of the term *stair horse*, finally he could stand it no longer, and enquired very earnestly, what I meant by stair horse in Orange County language, declaring he had never heard such a thing before in all his life, and could not see the analogy between a horse and a stair case. Some merriment was enjoyed at his expense, but not without making him a wiser man.

5061

PITCH BOARD.

Is a right angled triangle, and corresponds to the tread, riser and pitch, or inclination of the stairs.

HEIGHT ROD.

Is that, on which is divided the number of steps contained in each story, or flight of stairs (in height).

CYLINDER.

Is a round solid, having a circular base, equal and parallel.

HOLLOW CYLINDEr.

The face string of a winding stairs corresponding to well hole.

WELL HOLE.

A hollow cylinder, around which the steps pass and are supported.

HORSE.

The principal timber in a stair carriage, out of which the shape of the steps is cut.

CARRIAGE.

All the timbers, as a whole; that which supports the stair case.

WALL STRING.   Is the plank out of which is gained the shape of the steps, and fastened to the wall, whether straight or circular.

FACE STRING.   Is the outside, or face board of the steps and connects with the well hole.

FACE MOULD.   Is a pattern, used to cut out the rail timber, and is the principal mould used.

FALLING MOULD.   Is a pattern of the inside or outside edge of the rail, (used in this work) only to obtain the top line of the rail.

BOTTOM MOULD.   Is a mould used to mark the bottom of the rail, and is applicable to this work only, not being used in any other to my knowledge.

BUTT JOINT.   Is a joint made at right angles to the top of the rail and secured by a handrail screw.

EASMENT.	Is a curved line intersecting two straight lines, which form an angle.
SEGMENT.	Is as much of a circle, as is cut by a chord line.
SPIRAL.	Is circular passing around a centre, winding upwards, a twist line, and geometrically regular in its ascent.
GEOMETRICAL.	Is from Ge, the earth and Metron, the measure, belonging to laid down by, or disposed of according to principles of Geometry, and is divided into speculative and practical.
ELLIPTICAL.	Is oval not from a common centre, having a major and minor axis.
STRESS BLOCKS.	Are in spiral stairs, the blocks which support the carriage, and in winding stairs, what the horse is in straight ones.

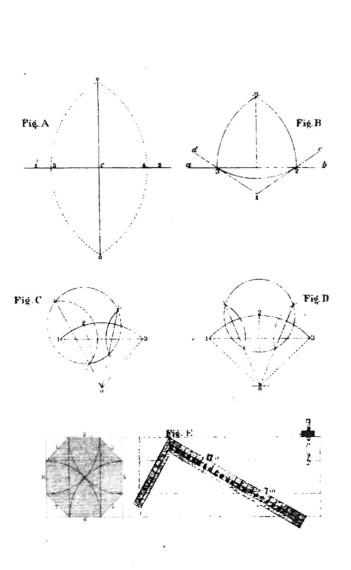

Fig.A

Fig.B

Fig.C

Fig.D

Fig.E

GEOMETRICAL PROBLEMS.

PLATE *A.*

Fig. A. To divide a line into two equal parts by a perpendicular.

Let 1, 3, 4, 2 be a given line, and 3, 4, the part to be divided, set a compass at 3 and 4 respectively and describe the arcs to intersect at *o, o,* draw through these points, which cuts the centre at *c.*

Fig. B. To describe any desired easment from a given angle.

Let 1 *d* and 1 *c* be the lines forming an angle, set the compass 1, 3 any length at pleasure, also 1, 2, draw *a b* through these points, describe from 3 and 2 the arcs to meet at *o,* set the compass at *o* and connect 3 and 2, which makes the easment.

Figs. C and D. To find a centre, ~~with~~
describe the segment of a circle, touching ~~any~~
given points.

Let 1, 2, 3 in both figures be points set at
random, or intentionally, as the case may be; then set
the compass at 2 and describe a circle, greater in diameter than half the distance between the two farthest
points, and without altering the compass, set at 1 and
3, and describe arcs intersecting the circle, through
these intersections draw lines until they meet as at *o*,
which will be the centre.

*Fig. E. To form an octagon from a square
piece of timber without laying it off on the end.*

Take a common 2 feet square, lay it on the timber
as seen in the figure, diagonally from side to side, and
at 7 or 17 inches put points to which strike the lines,
or set a guage. *)

---

*) This is a very simple method, and may be done without
sawing off the ends of the timber, any pieces under two feet wide
may be laid off in this way, but when the timber is larger, double the
proportion, say 4 feet and 14 inches and the length will be the same.
The latter method may be used in laying off the foundations of octagon
buildings &c.

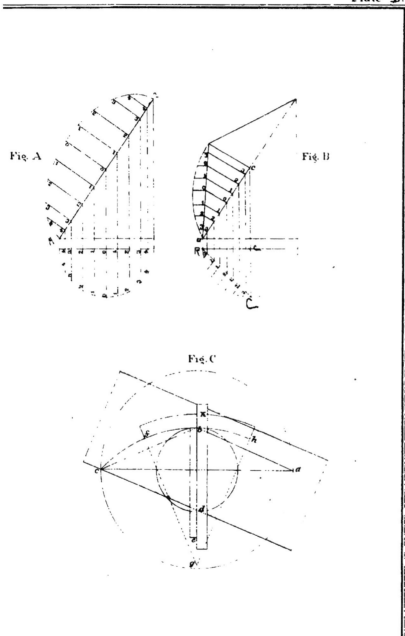

Fig. A

Fig. B

Fig. C

PLATE *B*.

SECTIONS OF A CYLINDER.

A cylinder, cut by any plane, through from one side to the other gives sections, which are elliptical, as seen in Fig. *A*. But a chord line of one quarter circle may be traced to produce the segment of a larger circle, as seen in Fig. *B*, when the distances are taken at right angles from the chord line in each case.

This latter plan applies to hand rails, and it is evident, the chord line should be formed in the manner here laid down, from the fact of the rail passing round the centre of the cylinder at equal distances from any point we please to measure.

Therefore *c*, *r*, being the distance from the centre to the inside edge of the rail, it must produce the chord line *r*, *a*.

This brings the true inside line of the rail very nearly, but the twist of the rail, when finished, makes it exactly right, and throws the radius of the greater circle on *r*, *c*, when elevated to its proper position on the stairs. See Plates 19 and 20.

The figures 1, 2, 3, 4 &c. indicate the distances from the chord line in each case, and are pointed off, from the plan below, on the greater circle or segment.

Fig. C. How to form the elliptic curve ...
any three given points in order to des...
quarter section of an ellipsis with a stick, as ...
Plate 7 *Fig. C.*

Let a, b, c represent the three points, and b, d ...
minor circle, then a, c will be the major circle, ...
circles corespond to the major and minor axes of ...
ellipsis. Now it is selfevident, that if the piece x ...
tacked on the plank to the line of the minor axis b, d, ...
a stick cut, the whole length to be b, d, e, (and the notch
b, d,) then keeping both corners tight to the plank and
drawing towards the left at c, it must describe the elliptic curve b, f, c, which is almost a perfect circle, and it
only begins to vary from a little to the right of f to c; the
distance b, h is equal to b, f or, f, c, showing it to be an
exact quarter circle of what is required. The stick is
made as follows : Cut the notch the length of b, d, and
the whole length of it from c, d, now if a centre at g were
found as on Pl. A Fig. D, it would show, how very close
to a segment of a larger circle the rail piece would come;
but as the spiral line, when worked on this segment,
fits the circle exactly, it is the true method of making
them for spiral rails, for the true inside line of a hand
rail on these kind of stairs is neither a true segment,
nor an ellipsis, but a spiral curve, and which must be
worked *from* the segment of a larger circle, (as the

Plate 1.

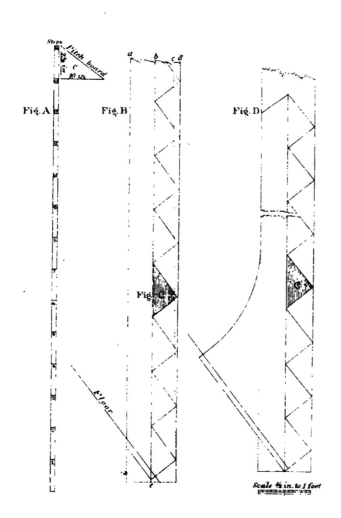

Fig. A

Fig. B

Fig. D

Steps

Pitch board

25 in.

C

10 in.

a   b   c d

Fig.

Floor

Scale ½ in. to 1 foot

spiral line runs diagonally on the inside of a segment), to make the twist.

This is the problem from which a thorough knowledge of hand rails can be obtained and should be studied carefully; it embraces the facts and reasons for adopting the plans in this treatise, it shows also, when carried out, the way to describe any kind of rail, whether spiral, or elliptical, to any height. The three points c, b, a and the line c, a, correspond to the chord line of the semi cylinder on Plate 19, to wit, b, f, a being the points on that figure, and b, e, a the chord line.

PLATE 1.

Fig. A. Is a rod including the height of the story from floor to floor and as shown. makes fourteen steps.

At the top fig. C is what is called a pitch board, showing the steps to be $7\frac{1}{4}$ inches high and 10 inches wide (which would be the cut of a horse, and of course, whatever would be allowed for nosing and finish would be extra from this for width). This right angle triangle gives the inclination or pitch of the stair case.

It is important to know the use, as well, as the methods, of getting the inclination of stair cases. Therefore let the manner of obtaing it be firmly fixed in the mind, before proceeding.

Fig. *B.* Represents a rough plank, [illegible] is to be cut a horse, for the support of the steps, [illegible] ing to the pitch board *C.* It will be seen that [illegible] may be of unequal width as at *c d.* The [illegible] the plank must be parallel to *b*, *e*, and is the line [illegible] followed in laying off the steps.

Fig. *D.* Is a face string fastened to the out[illegible] horse. The best way to do this, is to lay off [illegible] number of steps required, and then either saw [illegible] first, the face string , or fasten with nails or screws [illegible] the plank, and saw out both together, in this way if [illegible] springs it will not be of any importance, as they both must spring alike.

It is proper to remark here, that as no person can lay off two strings exactly alike with a pitch board, it is best to lay off the wall string, as explained on Plate 2, first, after which lay the board for the face string on it and point off all the steps, then lay the pitch board between every two points, and mark them on the face string, for should the face string be half an inch longer or shorter than the wall string, it would throw the stair case out of square, and cause much trouble in stepping them up.

Plate 2.

Fig.A.

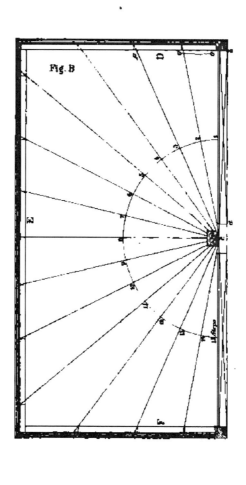

Fig.B

Scale ½ to 12 in

PLATE 2.

Fig. *A* shows how to make wall strings.

First make a pattern, the exact shape of the tread or nosing. Then place the pitch board *c* on the line *o, o,* and the pattern under it, and so mark off all the steps in the string. Then take a bit, in size to suit the thickness of the step, and bore a number of holes as *e, e, e, e,* at the bottom step, about ⅔ of an inch deep, run a guage on the back of the plank to suit the depth, and after dressing out *e, e, e, e,* nicely to the lines, use a small back saw, for cutting out the remainder, and so proceed with each step.

This is the best possible method of making wall strings, the old method of fitting them down after the steps are on, is out of date, although some persons practice this plan yet, for want of a better,. It makes also a much neater job, as by keying in the steps they may be made to fit exactly with scarcely any difficulty.

The treads and risers should be tounged together and glued. It is not essential however to tounge the back of the tread, as represented in the diagram, unless extra pains are to be taken with the work, as it might as well be nailed from the back side. But the riser, at the nosing, should be glued and also the scocia moulding when made and piled away ready for use. The space below and behind the riser and tread

2

shows the key room, the keys should be [illegible] glue or white lead.

Fig. *B*. Exhibits a general view of winding cases. These kind although often very clumsy nevertheless sometimes very useful, and indespensably necessary. They may be put up in a less space than is required for any other kind. First lay down on the floor the exact shape and size of the place to contain the stair. Then find the centre, allowing the necessary room for doors, if any, on each side, describe the circle 1, 2, 3 &c. in the centre of the tread, or thereabouts, on which point off the number of steps. Then draw from the centre, as at *c*, through the points, to the walls. The shaded lines 1, 2, 3, 4, at the wall are to represent boards planed off, which are to project above the horses, to finish on; *D*, *E*, *F* are the horses, cut in the following manner :

Lay the square on the board, and take the distance *o o* for the first tread, then make one height, reverse the square, and take again for the tread from *o* to *p*, add another rise, and so on to the end. In reversing the square, *Judgment* must be exercised or the cuts will run off the board, in case they do, the same must be persued until the cuts come so as to give the most strength in the carriage, these horses are then nailed

Plate 3.

Fig. A

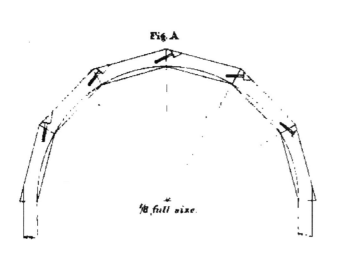

⅛ full size.

Fig. B

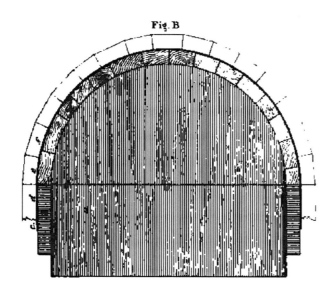

Plate 4.

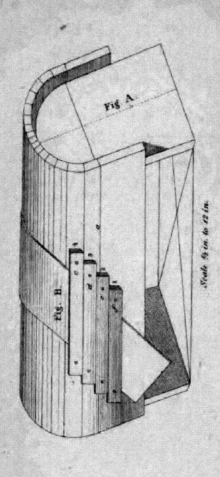

Fig A.

Fig. B.

Scale ½ in. to 12 in.

on the boards, already fastened to the wall, and the steps fitted to them.

When by practice, proficiency will suggest, the modes of keying them as in straight flights, previously described.

PLATE 3.

Fig. *A*. Exhibits a top view of a hollow cylinder or well hole, the manner of making them when no veneer is used, to obtain the width of the staves, and the amount of curvarture in each.

A better plan however is to plane out a veneer, as shown in Fig. *B* The veneer should be the width of the face string' and about ⅛ of an inch thick, it will then be pliable enough to bend around a tub made as shown in Figure *B*, Plate 4, without steaming or wetting.

Fig. *B* is a cylinder or tub, *d, e, f* the staves, *c* the veneer, *b* the staves of the tub and *a* its end.

PLATE 4.

Fig. *A*. This plate shows the manner of constructing a cylinder, *B* is the veneer passing over the tub, the staves *f e d c* are first fitted around the tub on the veneer, and screwed to it, after they are all

fitted number them, as shown, commence
one side putting each stave to its number,
ing about one day it will be ready for
persons have a fashion of wetting and steam
veneer but this is a bad practice, as it takes
length of time to dry, and often, it remains soft
time, and is more liable to be broken.

How to put the veneer on the tub, and have
right inclination.

Take the line *o*, (being the axis of the cylinder
and square across the bottom to the opposite side,
measure up as high, on that line, as you have height
to over come in passing around the circle, or well hole,
and bend the veneer to these points.

This holds good in relation to any kind of stairs
wether half a step or more are in the well hole, allways
being shure to have the tub long enough to suit the
height to be overcome. Another method of making
them is shown on plate 17 figure *B* (which see).

PLATE 5.

Exhibits a platform or carriage and may be used
for either a *Spiral* or *Elliptical* rail, the only difference
consisting in the manner of putting in the steps.

Plate 5.

Scale ½ in. to 1 foot.

Plate 6.

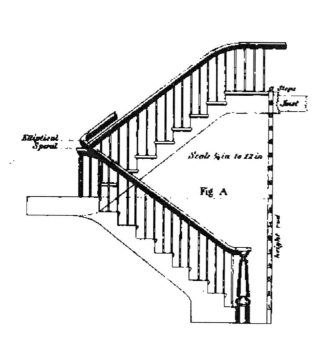

Elliptical Spiral

8 Steps

Joist

Scale ½ in to 12 in

Fig. A

height rod

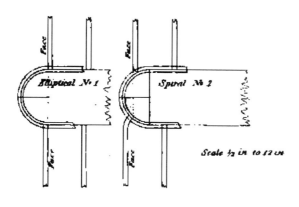

Face

Elliptical Nº 1

Face

Face

Spiral Nº 2

Face

Scale ½ in to 12 in

If the steps are put as *c* and *a*, the distance being greater around the well hole than one of the treads coming up below, it produces a falling, or lowering of the rail at the centre of the platform *g*, in a well hole of one foot, it becomes as seen in plate 6. Fig. *A.*

But to make a continued spiral rail, place the steps as at *f* and *e*, the distance around the tread will then be equal to any in the straight part, and of course the inclination of the rail the same, and no difference in the platform, except cutting the horses, at the top, where the pieces on each side of the well hole, are lettered *B, B.* Spike those against the platform, where a spiral rail is to pass over it.

PLATE 6.

Fig. *A.* Shows the difference, between a *spiral*, and an *elliptical rail* on a platform stair. The spiral, it will be seen, runs on in a continuous manner, and in consequence, would run one half step higher on the same stair case, than the elliptical. (See an explanation of the terms Plates 18, 19, 20.) But if the well hole is placed differently in the platform, the distance will be the same at all points from the nosings to the rail.

The plans below, No. 1, and No. 2, exhibit the different methods of placing them.

PLATE 7.

Here is shown the method of obtaining the mould, or pattern of the rail, for the elliptical rail Plate 5.

Make the circle a, c, f (Fig. A) to correspond exactly with the inside line of the rail, passing even and around it. Take the pitch board a, b, d, and measure from a, to the centre of the circle, or well hole, on the pitch board, then square up from the bottom at o, passing up the centre, and it will cut the *chord line*, or pitch line, at c.

Then take o, a as the minor, and c, a as the major axis of an ellipsis and by making a stick to correspond to these lengths as seen in Fig. C. An elliptic curve may be described in the manner laid down on Pl. 14, Fig B, which will be the exact inside line of the rail as seen in Fig. B, a, o, c.

The reason, a circle must be extended in length, without increasing its width, in passing around an elliptic curve, is plain, for if the distance a, o, be elevated to the inclination a, c, it looses, from i to c which is the same as from i to c in the ellipsis Fig. B, and the pitch line is what would be the major axis of an ellipsis, were a right cylinder cut by it. This holds good in all rails, which fall any below the inclination, or pitch, in passing around the well hole, wether they

Plate 7.

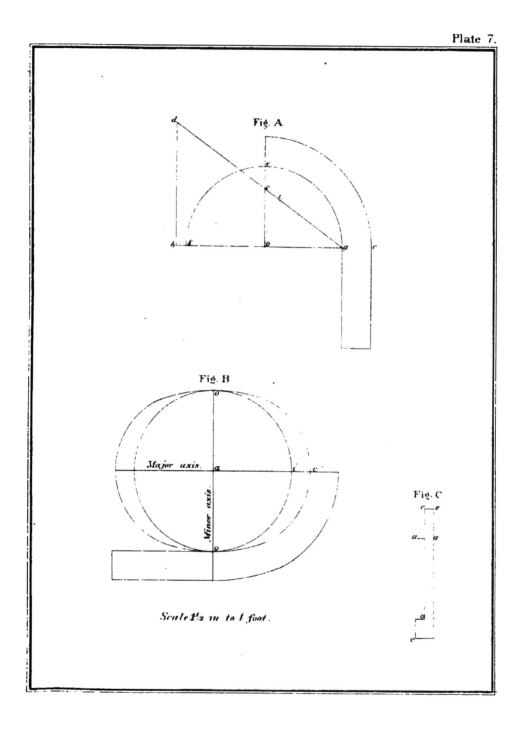

Fig. A

Fig. B

Major axis.

Minor axis.

Fig. C

Scale 1½ in to 1 foot.

Plate 8.

Fig. A

3 in. wide

Landing

Fig. B

Pitch

Pitch

Fig. C

Fig. D

contain one or more steps, but is never applicable where the inclination is *spiral* or continuous, and without easment.

PLATE 8.

Exhibits the method of working the rail for an elliptic stair case.

The rail timber being cut square through from the face of the plank.

Place the pattern of the rail on the piece as seen in Fig. *A*, the long side of the pitch board on a plain with the face of the rail piece. The dotted lines, show the centre and outside of the rail; the one passing through its centre shows, that the pattern may be raised or lowered to suit the thickness of timber, provided, the same amount is taken from the other end so as to give the rail the same inclination when finished, as seen in the diagram. By this method a moulded rail of 2 inches in thickness, may be worked from a piece of timber $2\frac{1}{4}$ inches thick, for a well hole of one foot diameter, and a round rail requires no more than just its thickness of timber.

A good manner of working rails and applying moulds and patterns, is to screw the rail piece into the vice, and elevate it to the back of the pitch board by

placing it on the bench, (if level) then the
level, and level across the end, put the rail
right angles, or plumb under it.

This is what corresponds to the level on the
landing, in passing around the well hole, the two
must be worked from one end, as it always should in
elliptical rails, for it is evident, if the rail piece is sprung
or in any way altered from its original position, it
alters the curvature, and can no longer follow the
intended circle.

To work the return twist apply the pattern the
reverse way and proceed as before, it will be seen also
that the rail, when finished, is precisely the same, as
though it had been worked by the old methods, according to the pitch lines.

How to work the rail:

In cutting square through from the face of the
plank, the top edge of a falling mould is only used,
but for getting the thickness of the rail, a pair of compasses may be altered at the points, as represented by
Fig. *D*. Therefore when the top of the rail is worked,
the under side may be scribed off accurately by these
compasses from the top side.

Plate 9.

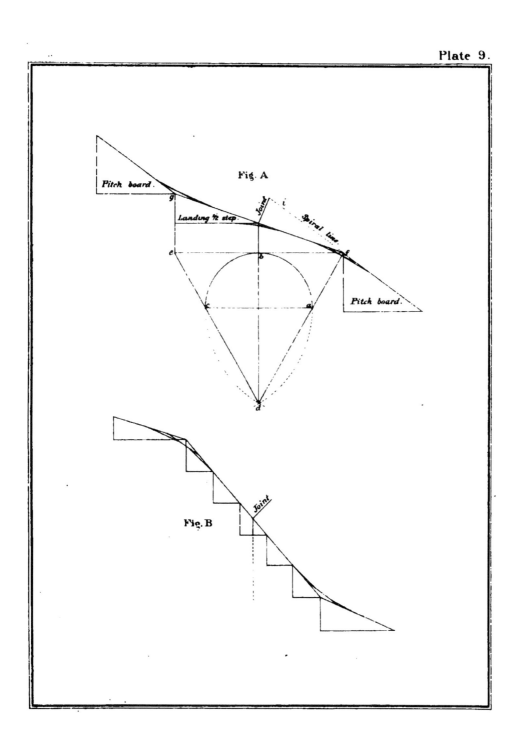

Fig. A

Pitch board.

Landing ½ step.

Joint

Spiral line

Pitch board.

Fig. B

Joint

. Suppose the top of the rail to be worked, according to the desired twist, then place the face mould, on it and mark all which is to come off, from the top square the rail piece to this line, and scribe the thickness outside and inside.

Cut another mould to correspond to the bottom of the rail, as seen in Plate 13, marked *x*, apply it to the bottom in the same manner as the top one, work to these lines, and it gives a rail shaped as Fig. *C*, Plate 13, after which any desired shape may be given.

Fig. *B* exhibits the manner of making easments by intersectional lines, the retrogressive steps, on a platform stairs, form an angle as in this figure, and the rail should always run one half step higher on the landing, or be made to suit the height of the long balusters.

Fig. *C* represents the easment on a newel post.

PLATE 9.

How to draw falling moulds.

Fig. *A* gives the shape of the rail, when placed over the circle, or what is commonly called a falling mould.

Let *a, b, c* represent the exact inside, or outside line of the rail, according to the kind of mould to be obtained, set a compass from *a* to c (the diameter of the circle) and describe the dotted lines from *c* to *d*, and from *a* to *d*, draw from *d* through *a* and *c*, to *e* and *f*, make *e, f* parallel to *a, c*, and at right angles erect the height to be overcome in passing around the well hole or circle of the rail, as *e, g*, then draw the line *g, f*, place the pitch boards at right angles to *e, g*, and *e, f*, when any desired easment may be drawn by the intersection of lines, or by compasses to suit the eye. Make the butt joint at right angles from *g, f*, in the centre.

The dotted line shows what is denominated the *spiral* line, wherein there is no easment, but a continual twist.

When the rail passes on a landing or floor, where the flight runs from floor to floor, a small easment should be made at the centre, which is one half step higher than the rail coming up from below.

Fig. *B.* Another method is to lay off the steps around the inside or outside of the rail, this is where more than one step is in the circle, as seen in the figure.

Care must be taken, in laying it down to have the exact pitch of the steps for the inside of the rail,

Plate 10.

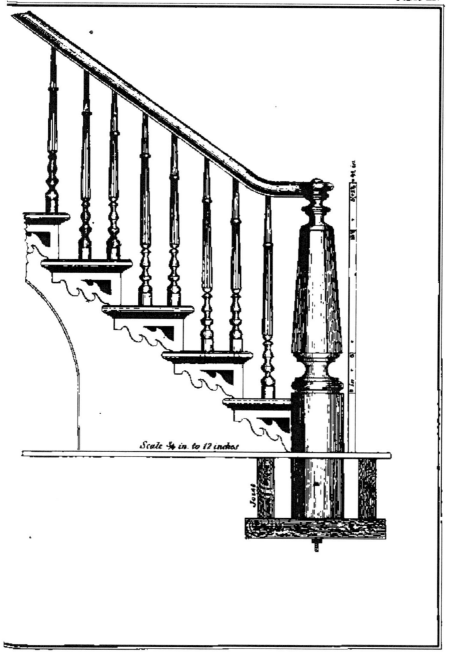

Scale ¾ in. to 12 inches

when getting an inside mould, and for the outside when getting an outside mould. This is a very natural and comprehensive way of getting a mould; the true pitch should be ascertained, and a pitch board made, when it may be passed along a board and the number of steps marked on it; also the different pitches eased into each other, and the mark for the holes pointed off on the mould, for boring the rail.

Boring the Rail.

As a general thing two balusters are placed on a step, and to find the distance from centre to centre, divide the base line of the pitch board equally, then square up from the bottom and the pitch line will be cut in the centre also; therefore half the length of the pitch line is the distance between the holes for the balusters on the rail.

Points should be taken on a rod, both to make the rail and also to divide off the holes, but by experience it may be avoided, as a good stair builder would make an entire stair case, without even seeing the building had he only the pitch and number of steps required. But for beginners this is the best method, the rail may be then bored, by dividing the balusters along the rail between these points.

28

Sometimes the rail may be laid on the nosings and the holes marked on it by squaring up from the steps.

A good plan however for the twist part is, to bore it after it is strung over the circle, when it may be marked correctly by plumbing up from the steps.

Newel Posts.

PLATE 10.

Exhibits part of a stair including the newel post. The proper method of making them, where a good solid one can not be obtained, and also where they may be preferred, on account of beauty and durability:

The height rod at the side of the post, shows the different parts of which it is made up; the base below is generally about 9 inches, the mouldings between it and the spire, as also between the spire and top, are simply two pieces of the rail plank glued together, and turned in a lathe to suit the fancy.

The spire and base are veneered with the kind of wood of which the rail and balusters are made, a screw, passing through the rail cap and post below the joist, is fastened in the manner seen on the diagram.

Plate II.

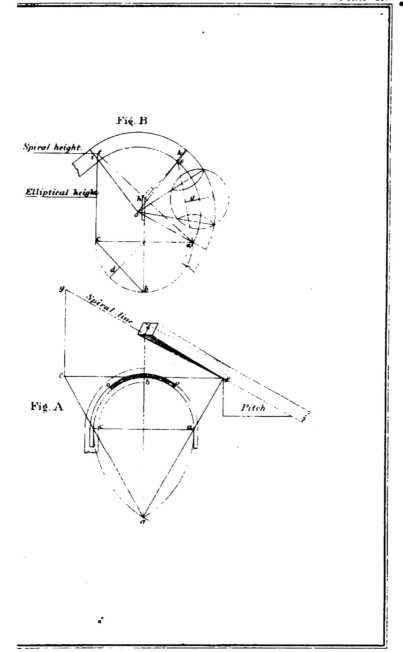

Fig. B

Spiral height.

Elliptical height

Fig. A

Spiral line

Pitch

By this means the post may be fastened much firmer than by keys, and should it at any time become loose, may be screwed up at pleasure.

A good way to cut the dovetails in the steps is also here shown, by cutting one side square, a nail may be driven in and the step firmly secured to the face string without showing it as the baluster covers it when in.

The face string should be finished down in the manner here described, where it is practicable, as it is much neater, than when connecting the base without an easment. *)

PLATE 11.

I am now about to explain the method of getting out rails by a plan never before published, and which

---

*) As stated in the introduction, it is not deemed necessary to give the manner of making curtail steps and rails in this volume, as it would be a repetition only and of no benefit. Nearly all the numerous works published on this subject, contain the manner of constructing them.

is contrary to all the ideas, it has be... examine, by all authors I have met wit... as before stated, the principal reason ... book to the public.

Fig. *A.* By this plan the falling mou... obtained, or at least the outstretch of the circle... and the pitch applied, in order to ascertain the ... height, to be overcome in going around the circle,... inside line of the rail.

Therefore let *a, b, c* be the exact line of the well hole. Then divide half the step, or base line of the pitch board, each way from the centre or plumb line, which is indicated by the shaded part *o, o.* Find the stretchout as on Plate 9. Place the pitch board, as usual, at right angles from *e* and *f*, continue the pitch line, then erect the perpendicular *e, g.*

This gives a line from which to construct the falling mould, also the exact height the rail will attain in passing over and around the well hole.

At right angles from the pitch line, and in the centre, draw the thickness of the rail, then measure on each side half the width of the rail. Connect these lines with the pitch board, and it gives the falling mould inside and outside.

The easment on the rail is so slight, that any judgment on the part of the workman would dispense with the use of a falling mould, except for the purpose of marking the joint on the rail.

Fig. B. *How to find the face mould for a spiral rail.*

Let *a, b, c* be the exact inside line of the rail, found by the falling mould, draw the chord line in the circle *c, b*, erect *d* in its centre.

Erect the perpendicular *c, e*, equal in height to the spiral line at *g*, in Fig. A. Draw the chord line from *e to a*, plumb up from the centre of the well hole *b, h*, to the chord line *e, a*, and at right angles make *f* equal in length to half the diameter of the circle, draw a chord line from *f* to *a*, in the centre of which and at right angles to it make *g*, equal to *d* in the plan below.

This then gives the points f, g, [...]
at the point g, and describe a circle aro[...]
¾ the distance from a and f, then without [...]
compasses put the foot at a and f, and describe [...]
to intersect, now draw through these inters[...]
lines to the centre at o, from whence describe the in[...]
line of the rail, a, g, f. To make the butt joint, [...]
lines from o through a and f. From o, a at right an[...]
extend the length of the straight part of the rail [...]
pleasure. The mould should be made a little longer [...]
in order to have wood to make the joint exact.

From the same centre may be described, a si[...]
milar mould to i, but as it is the segment of a larger
circle, the same pattern may be used continuously
right and left.

It will be seen, that the mould falls below the
point e at i. This is owing to the twist required in
the rail, as each piece revolves on the points a and f;
and when it is worked will throw the rail to its proper
height, (see Plate 13, Figs. A, B, C, for a full explanation; also Plates 18, 19 and 20.)

The bevel taken from lines b, h and f to work the
twist is applied on the plank from the inside and out-

Plate 12.

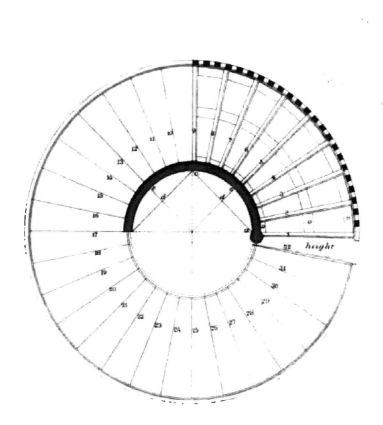

Scale ¼ in. to 12 in.

side of the timber, *on both ends*, which is cut square through from its face, as on Plate 13 (which now read carefully).

PLATE 12.

Exhibits a Spiral or Geometrical Stairs, a continuation of winders from bottom to top.

The numbers 32 indicate the number of steps in the circle, the shaded part the rail; *o, o, o* are *stress blocks*, and are the principal pieces in the construction of the carriage; *c, d, a* show the chord line of one quarter part of the circle, from which is found (by the previous method) the rail, one mould being sufficient for all the segments in the circle. See Plate 17 how to build the carriage and wall string *)

The carriage, rail, wall string, &c. are invariably got in the same manner, as described on the plates referred to above.

---

*) This plate contains the principles of all spiral stairs and rails, and any alteration is only a variation from the general rule.

PLATE 18.

How to find the face mould of ..... the easiest possible manner, for spiral ....

Let a, e, f, Fig. A be the exact inside line of rail, draw the chord line e, b, f, and at the centre, draw out the line b, to the circle. Erect a perpendicular from the axis of the circle on a, e, equal in height to half the number of steps in coming around the circle over which the rail is to pass. (1, 2, 3, 4 or 5, being heights in the quarter circle) Then draw the line to .... At right angles from o, produce c, equal in length to half the axis a, e, from c draw the line to a, which corresponds to e, b, f in the plan, make b also in the same manner as below.

This gives the points a, b, c; then take any thing more than one half the distance between b and a, or c, and describe a circle, placing the foot of the compasses respectively at c and a, making intersecting circles, and through these points draw lines to the centre G, from where describe the inside line of the face mould a, b, c. This is the same method as Plate A Fig. C and D.

Plate 13.

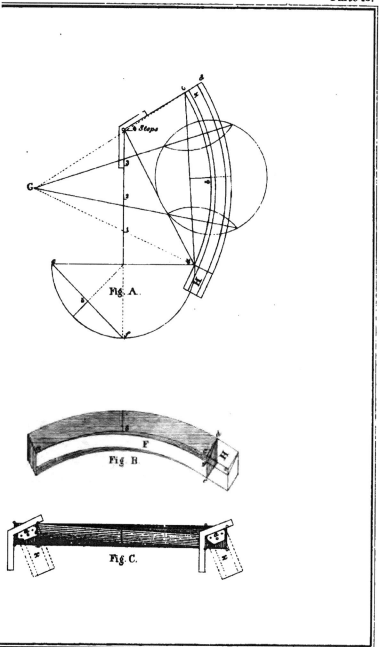

Fig. A.

Fig. B.

Fig. C.

The lines represented on the mould marked x, make a mould from the same centre for the bottom of the rail, c, d, is the width of the mould.

Make both joints by drawing lines from G through a and c, and any length of timber required for an easment, extend at right angles from G, a, indicated by H.

The bevel taken from the diagram is applied as seen on Fig. C.

Fig. B exhibits a piece of rail timber, from the saw, perfectly square, and just the width of the rail, except $\frac{1}{16}$ of an inch allowed for smoothing up.

H, is the straight part attached to the twist for the easment. a, b, c, the inside line. c, d its width, and c, e the depth of it. F is a piece of paste board which represents the falling mould (but for continuous twists, all that is used is a piece straight on its edge.)

Fig. C exhibits, only the inside and ends of a similar piece, the square ends shown by the pattern of the rail, and the bevel taken from Fig. *A*, applied on the inside of one end and the outside of the other.

There is no straight part to this, and therefore would be such as is made for continuous winders, each successive piece being but a continuation of the same pattern.

It will be observed, that the line across the timber representing the shape of the rail, is elevated somewhat more than the face mould naturally throws it, this is owing to the twist which must be worked on the timber, and when the rail is placed in its position over the well hole, will be exactly right in height and otherwise.

By refering to Plates 11 and 19 it will be seen also, that the circle of the inside line of the rail, when continued around the cylinder seems less in height than the number of steps would require, but this is owing to the manner of viewing the line, as it cannot be represented on paper exactly. For if the circle were drawn through the right angled point of the chord line (which represents the axis of the cylinder in those figures) it would appear too narrow at the centre of the quarter circle.

The doted lines are the plumb lines, supposing it were cut according to the pitch, which it is not but still show it to be the same when finished as though it were cut in that way.

How to work a twist for a spiral rail.

Dress the rail timber perfectly square from its face, just the width of the rail, (allowing a little to smooth up) apply the falling moulds or mold, only to obtain the top of the rail, and easment if any.

Apply the bevel on the outside and inside edge of the rail, as in Fig. C according (to wether it is to run right or left handed) work off the top to the top lines of the rail piece, the rail remains square in the middle of the piece and the twist runs both ways, but still the middle will be reduced by the inside and outside lines.

Then take the face mould again and lap it on the rail piece marking all on the outside, and being shure to keep it on the inside edge of the timber, or as the patterns on the ends of the piece require. Then work of this wood at right angles from the top of the rail. Now take the compasses described on Plate 8, and set them to the desired thikness of the rail, and scribe off the inside and outside, Work to these lines, Then place the bottom mould in its proper position, (the centre of the rail) and mark both sides, work of these to lines, and it gives the shape of the rail as at *a*. Plate 13, Fig. *C.*

After which any other shaped rail may be worked out of it to suit the fancy.

For a round rail the corners may be guaged off from the square piece, and worked as if it were a straight rail.

INTRODUCTORY REMARKS CONCERN- ING SPIRAL AND ELLIPTICAL LINES FOR HAND RAILS.

I have mentioned before, that in some cases it is necessary to cut out the face moulds on the elliptical plan, (introduced by Peter Nicholson many years ago) but nothing can be more void of principle, than many of the plans laid down, in regard to spiral rails. And it seems as though no pains have been taken by any later authors to correct the mistake, as they have based their investigations on the theory of cutting a cylinder to the required pitch, supposing the elliptical section, thereby given, to be the true inside line of the rail, in passing over and around the well hole.

The only difficulty with those authors, seems to have been, that, of disputing the correctness of the above named theory, thereby coming in contact with established rules and opinions, but I would ask; *How is it possible to advance in the arts and siences,* without coming in contact, and successfully removing from the mind, erroneous theories, it matters not by whom, or how long established.

40

It is true many books have been published set-
ing forth improvements made in handrails, but still,
being based on the same old theory, to me at least,
it has been a different reading of the same book.

Therefore I assert there have been no real improvement since to my knowledge, and this being the
proper place, I will endeavour to explain (in a short
way) the difference between a spiral and an elliptical line.

The spiral line passing around, the cylinder is
regular and continuous in its inclination, whereas the
elliptic shortens and quickens around its major axis,
and while the spiral line continues to run on up like
the screw of an auger, the elliptical line, after passing
its major axis, actually runs down the opposite side,
of the cylinder as it necessarily must, in forming the
elliptical section.

Therefore where an easment is wanted, as on a
landing, the elliptical line is just the thing required.

Plate 14.

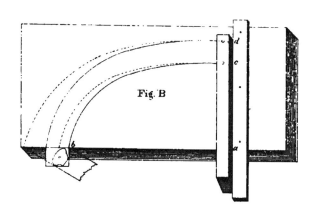

Fig. B

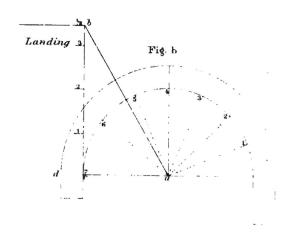

Landing

Fig. b

41

PLATE 14.

How to describe one fourth of an ellipse with a stick as shown on Plate 7:

This stick represents half the major and minor axes of the ellipse.

It will be seen that the well hole here laid down contains 4 steps to the centre, and but 3 from it to the end of the circle, therefore it is plain, the rail should drop a little, to correspond with the nosings in height, but as the long balusters are always used on the landing, it is raised one half step, making it $3\frac{1}{2}$ steps high. Make the stick in Fig. *B* from the end to the extreme length, equal to *a*, *b*, in Fig. *b* below, and for the short diameter, from *a* to *c*, Fig. *b.*

Fig. *B* shows the manner of describing the face mould; the paste board which is intended for it, is laid on the plank or workbench, and a small stick tacked at right angles from the edge, the stick is then slipped tight to the angle and moved to the left or right according to the way the rail is to run; *a*, *c*, *d* show the distances on the stick, *a*, *c* the minor axis

and to *d* the width of the rail, shows the
stick passing below the strips, tacked on
therefore when the stick is moved, it
brougt into the circle, and makes the quarter

The pattern is then applied at right angles from
the short side of the pitch board, as described in
Plate 8, which it is presumed, the reader has acquainted himself with ere this.

Any of the moulds may be applied for any rail,
herein treated of, as well by the pitch lines, as by
cutting square through from the face of the plank,
but there is no danger of any one resorting to the old
method of cutting out rails with a whipsaw, when they
may be cut out by a jigsaw, in half the time, and besides, afterward worked in less time, than it would require, *even to cut them out by the old method.* The
dotted line on the outside of this mould shows what
it should be to cut the pitch.

The curvature of any part of an ellipse is altered
by twisting it out of its original position, therefore it
will not answer to work the twist from both ends, as
on a spiral rail piece, at least to be consistent with

Plate 15.

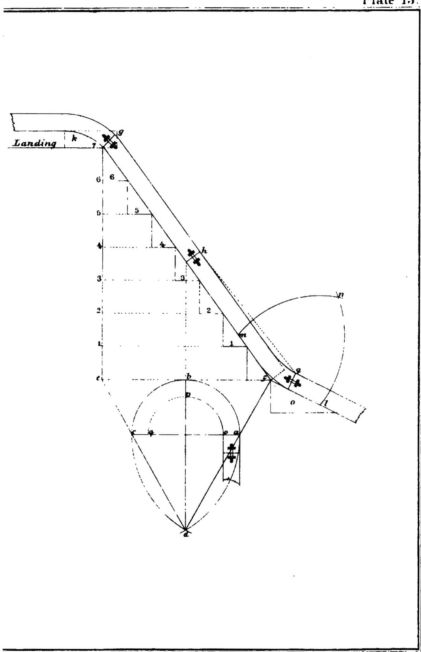

Landing

principle, if the inside of a rail were but the double section, cut by a given plane.

PLATE 15.

How to get a falling mould, showing the connections of straight rail, wether the steps are equal in number or the treads alike in width.

Lay off the plan of the rail *a, b, c,* if for the outside, and *o, p, q,* if the inside is required.

Obtain the stretchout of the semi circle, as given on Plate 9, then erect a perpendicular on the left hand side of the stretchout point, equal in height, to all the steps in the semi circle, counting from the bottom upward. From this point draw a line to the right hand point of the stretchout at *f.* Make the pitch board below (if any straight connects) at right angles from *e, b, f,* and the easments, by intersection of lines, or by making points *m, l* on the pitch lines, and setting the foot of the compasses to these points respectively describing *n,* from which make the easment. The letters *g, h, q* show the rail joints.

44

Care should be taken to make the easments as graceful, as the thickness of timber and other circumstances will admit, however the judgment of the workman has all to do in this matter, *as it regards taste.*

The easment at the top, it will be seen, is made by glueing the block *k* on the bottom of the straight part, and is a very good method, provided a little care be taken in working the rail piece exact, and also letting in the bolt.

It saves also, a good deal of trouble in making the upper twist.

It applies particularly to the kind on Plate 16, where the upper part of the rail is elliptical. But even on these the upper part may be made from the lower mould, by dropping the rail slightly, if it is preferred.

The straight part usually attached to the circular part of a rail, is from 3 to 8 inches, where it is proper to make the easment very long however, part of it should be made on the straight rail, as this saves thickness of timber in making the twist.

Plate 16.

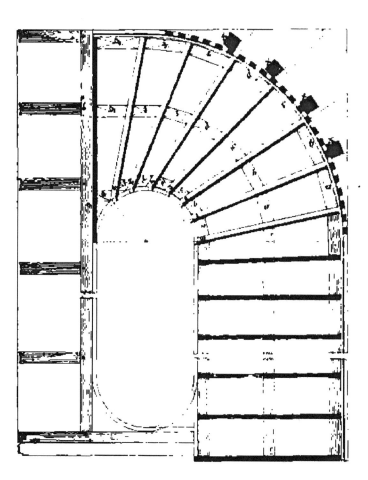

Scale ½ in to 1 foot.

45

If the rail starts from a newel post to wind continuously, the first piece should be got out, as shown on Plate 14, Fig. *b* and *B*.

It would not be essential to mark the steps on the diagram as here represented, but it is merely to show the similarity between this, and a plan for getting the same on Plate 9.

PLATE 16.

Exhibits a stair carriage showing the manner of constructing carriages of this kind generally.

Lay down on the floor the necessary lines, over which to build the stair carriage, as regards the number of steps, size of the well hole, position of the steps, rail, wall string, studding and stress blocks.

How to construct the stairs.

If a part of the carriage is straight, as in the diagram, commence putting up first, by placing the wall string of the straight part to its place and fastening it.

To this spike up the first rough
carriage as marked No. 10, or fasten it as
the case may be, place also the studding so also
as shown at x, x, x, x, and prop up the rough
at the well hole exactly plumb over the
the floor.

Then put up the next rough riser, one
higher in the circle than the first, and make the
blocks the tops of which are. a, a, a, &c. and the
cut as in Fig. A, Plate 17, (the sides of the blocks
marked b, b, showing the rough risers as they run one
above an other) then spike them into their places as
seen here also.

The rough risers should run into the circle so as
to cut them off plumb with the well hole in order to
nail the hollow cylinder at each step, as it increases
the strength of the carriage very much when finished,
and so proceed round spiking the rough risers to the
studding and letting them run on to the wall as seen
here. It is better on this account to have studding
placed here, than if a circular wall were built.

The studding generally should be left run to the
full hight of the building, sometimes however this

Plate 17.

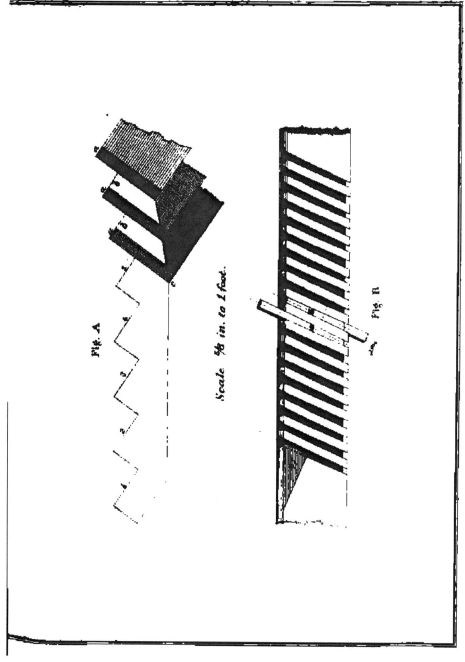

Fig. A.

Scale ⅜ in. to 1 foot.

Fig. B.

would not answer as the plan of the building might require the stairs to run to the hight of one story only.

Where they are left run the full height, a segment of the same circle should be placed at the top joists, and nailed through into the tops of the studding, but where they only run one story, the floor may be cut to the same circle, and the nosing and bulasters continued around as on landings.

The way to get the depth of the rough false riser is seen in Plate 17, Fig. *A*, where the straight part coming up from below is attached to it, viz: By cutting down through the horse, and adding to this length one rise in height. The bottom edge is afterward trimmed off to make the easment in the carriage, *a, a, a,* shows the rough risers in the carriage and *b, b,* are the stress blocks. *a, c* being the depth of the risers.

How to put down the wall string.

PLATE 17, Fig. *B*.

Shows the manner of making wall strings by keying them out of a plank.

The dove tails are cut diagonally across the plank according to a pitch board found from this line of the carriage, a plow bit is generally run on the top edge of the plank about $\frac{1}{2}$ inch deep and from $\frac{3}{8}$ to $\frac{1}{2}$ inch from its face, which is intended to receive a moulding, when plastered.

The keys should be cut as far through, as to the bottom of this groove, as seen in the figure.

How to get the pitch line.

Divide off on the inside line of the keys, *into spaces of about one inch*, the distance from the face of one riser to the face of the next, in the floor plan.

Take this distance as a base line, and square up one step, draw the *Hypothenuse* line, of the right angle, which gives the exact pitch of the string, as on the figure which is marked *C*.

It will be seen the keys are driven alternately from each side, this is in order to obviate the difficulty of springing one side too much.

A bevel may be set to the pitch board, and the centre lines marked on the plank about three inches apart, when the bevel should be again altered slightly, and the taper of the keys again marked, then saw out to the bottom of the groove on these lines.

The keys should be made about 4 inches longer than the dovetail, to allow for driving, and nearly square, for when the plank is sprung it makes the dovetails square, as marked on the Plate 16. Spring the plank to the studding, when it is ready for cutting down to its place, if the plank is moistened with hot water it will spring all the better, but requires time again to dry, befor fastening the joints.

How to cut it down.

Keep the wall string at both ends equal distance, when sprung, from the false risers, against the studding or wall, and mark plumb all the faces of the risers and joints to be made, then take down the string and cut them out, as marked, when it is ready to be placed in its position on the carriage.

In most cases when stairs are built in this way, the steps and risers are scribed up neatly to the wall string and so fastened permanently, but they may

be fitted to the string and marked, after which the
string is taken down and the steps gained out, or with
care, the pitch board may be run on the wall string
before being sprung, and the steps laid off, the same
as on a straight piece.

Well Holes.

May be made also by ascertaning the exact pitch in
the manner described on Plate 17, and by finding the
exact height they are to travel in passing around any
circle, for small cylinders or well holes, it is an inferior
method to the one laid down on Plate 4, and should
not be used, but for large well holes, it is preferable
on account of the shortness of time required in making them.

In well holes from 3 to 8 feet diameter, the keys
come from 3 to 5 inches apart, and the string may be
sprung to the carriage, thereby saving the time required
to make a well tub, generally a cutting thrust, or dado
plane, is used in cutting the depth of the gaines, and
afterward dressed out to receive the keys. *)

---

*) This kind of stair are preferable to any other kind for private
dwellings on account of their graceful appearance and adaptation to a

51

Many different methods are laid down for the construction of stair carriages, but as the method just described is considered the best as well, as the most expeditious for this kind, it is given, leaving the workman to consult his own judgment for variety.

Sometimes straight horses are used to run across the carriage instead of stress blocks, when these are used they may be cut by the same rule given on Plate 2, but to give an opinion, they are not near so permanent as the blocks.

---

front hall, also for economy in room, and by landing at once on the second floor, thereby forming no obstruction in passing to any room from the upper landing either way, front or back, and affording a passage way below in either direction, which a platform, would not admit, besides requiring much less room on the first floor.

5061

69.+ F -1-

Reasons For Adopting These Meth... In Making Hand Rails And The Phi... losophy Of The System, Explain... *Comparatively With Model...*

Although it might not be essentially necessary to have a complete knowledge of the principles involved in the preceeding rules, to succeed in working hand rails (from the plainess of the diagrams accompanying them). Yet, as the investigating mind demands a satisfactory explanation of the *Why and Wherefore*, it is thought proper to give these additional reasons; and as no better way exist to fasten conviction upon the mind, than by models, it is asked from those wishing to pursue the investigation further, to provide themselves with a small model, as follows:

PLATE 18.

Make a right cylinder about eight inches long and three inches in diameter, draw on both ends

Plate 1

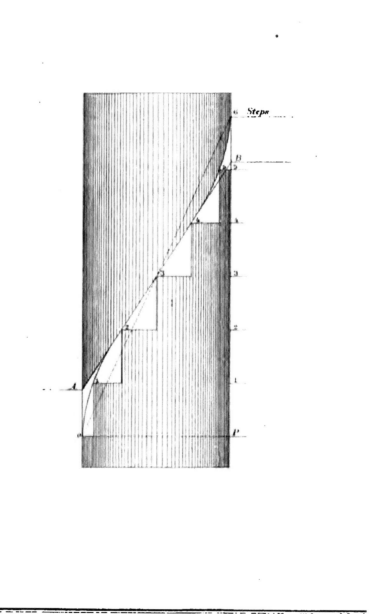

the axis lines, so as to divide it into two equal parts, then draw lines down each side connecting the axes, space off, say six steps high up one line, and divide half the cylinder in six parts also, this when the lines are drawn up and around it will form steps. Then take a strip of paper perfectly straight on its edge, and lap around the semi cylinder from the first step to the top, as seen on the figure from *a* to *b*. It will be seen, that this paper will follow all the points of the steps as 1, 2, 3, 4, 5 and 6, therefore this must be the spiral line and which a hand rail should follow.

Now if the line *A*, *B*, were cut through from side to side, it would pass 2, 3 and 4, but would fall short between 1, 2 and 4, 5, and if a line from *o* to 6, were cut it would touch o, 3, 6. It is evident this could not be the line of the rail. It is equally plain that no cut of a cylinder from any pitch, will suit a spiral line, for as already stated the section thus obtained must be elliptical, (therefore it is not true, that a hand rail is a double section of a cylinder cut by a given pitch) when used for spiral stairs, as contended for by P. Nicholson and later authors. For instead of being the double section of a cylinder it must be worked from the segment of a larger circle.

54

On page 18 of the new carpenters guide, may be found the following remarks:

"Upon these figures, meaning the cut of a cylinder any direction to make an *obstuse* angle with the plane of a segment". Depends the whole principles of hand rails for stairs, "The reader ought to understand how to form the sections of a cylinder in any case whatever, *for the face or raking mould of a hand rail, is nothing but the double section of a cylinder, &c.*

Contrary however to this general opinion here *Quoted*. I assert, that although by cutting a right cylinder to any pitch, from one side to another, its sections being elliptical, it does not follow that such sections are the true line of a spiral rail in passing around it, and more than this, it is a contradiction of terms to say, that the spiral line of a hand rail is elliptical, because, spiral is not elliptical.

I do not dispute the fact, that to cut a cylinder by any pitch its sections will be elliptical. But that an ellipsis although it fit a circle, will not pass regularly over the stairs and be an equal distance from the nosings, as it evidently should. On Plates 19 and 20

Plate 19.

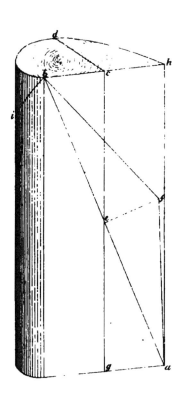

will be seen a further demonstration of these ideas
and the falacy of the elliptical theory of hand rails.

PLATE 19.

Shows a semi cylinder perspectively and corresponds to a well hole around which a hand rail passes.

Now let b, d, h, be the exact inside line of the
rail, then b, e, a, would be the chord line, if the cylinder were cut by the pitch, and it will be admitted,
that the rail passing around and over the well hole
should be equal distance, from a plumb line passing
up to the ceiling from the centre of the well hole, this
line would correspond to g, e, c, and b, i, shows the
spiral line passing around. Therefore the distance
c, d, must be made at right angles from the chord line
of one quarter circle, as the rail is made in two peices
for a semi circle.

Is it not evident then, that a, e, cannot be the
right length of a chord line for one quarter circle, as
the rail does not curve to the centre of the cylinder,
but keeps half the diameter of the inside line from it
in passing up and around.

56

PLATE 20.

Exhibits the same by ordinates, it will be observed that the distance b, a, is the same as c, d in Pl. 19.

By dividing the chord line of the quarter circle below into 8 parts or more, and plumbing up to the chord line d, b, e, and squaring from thence to the chord line of the cylinder d, a, and squaring from that again at random, then applying the distances from the quarter circle below on these lines, it gives points, which if connected will be the same as seen on Plate 13, and proven to be a segment of a larger circle by placing a compass at f.

This therefore is the true method of getting a rail piece by ordinates, wether the *plan* be elliptical or circular, but for the inside of an elliptical rail, it is the best method, and for the spiral mould take Plate 13. Where an easment is required as at a landing on spiral stairs, the above method is recommended, except, that the *plan* should be laid down as on Plate 14 or by the small stick on Plate 7, Fig. *C*, and Plate *B*, Fig. *C*.

Again, suppose as an illustration, a common *Screw Pump* be taken. The outside of the shaft around which the spiral line runs, is just the same as shown

Plate 20.

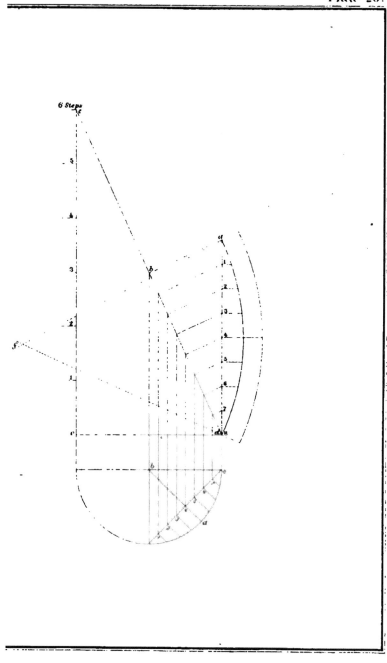

on Plate 19, and the straight strip which is used to lay off, the gaines or the twisted groove, is identical with the falling mould of a rail for the continuous part of the flight. A pump maker would laugh at the idea of stricking out these flights or parts of the twist, with a trammel, or by ordinates, and yet it would be no more absurd, than to use the same instrument, for a rail which evidently runs precisely the same on these kind of stairs.

A twist cut rifle will illustrate what I mean also, and has led me to introduce a problem, and a mathematical *Theorem*, for the solution of all such questions, I do this to gratify a class of individuals who may probably feel the necessity of a mathematical demonstration.

Suppose a rifle ball one half inch in diameter,
once round in passing 6 feet, the barrel being
long, and the distance to travel 100 yards. What distance would a mark travel on the outside of the ball.

Solution.

Take the circumferance of the semi diameter of
the ball, then suppose a right angle triangle, the base
line to be the length of this semi circumference, and
its perpendicular the length of the barrel, now by
drawing the hypothenuse the figure is complete. Then
by multiplying the hypothenuse line by 100 yards it
must give the exact distance the mark would travel,
hence the following *theorem.*

*The hypothenous of a right angle triangle is equal
to the spiral line of a semi cylinder, the outretch of which
is taken for the base line of the triangle. (See Plate* 21.)

Again, as the difference between a spiral and
elliptical line is considerable, I here give the way to
get the length of each, which shows conclusively, that
they cannot be taken for the same in any case whatever.

Plate 21.

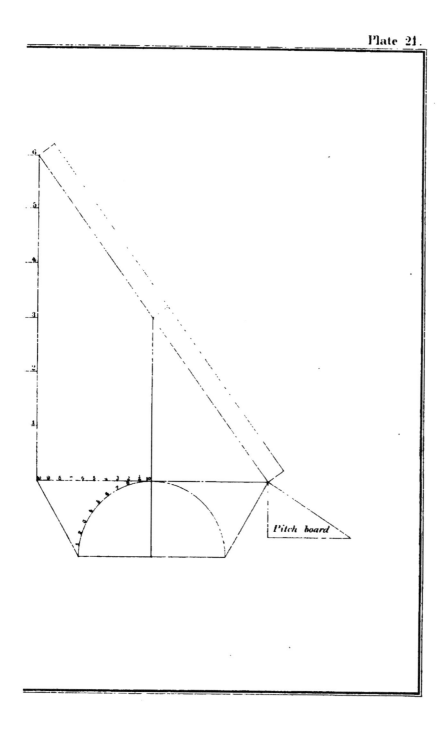

Pitch board

59

Rule for the spiral line.

The hypothenuse of a right angle triangle is equal to the square root of the sum of the squares of the **Base** and perpendicular lines, or thus by formula,

$$H = \sqrt{B^2 + P^2} \;\; ^*)$$

Rule for the elliptical line or arc.

The square root of half the sum of the squares of the major and minor axes, multiplied by 3, 1416, equals the circumference, or the ellipse, therefore one half of this must be the length of the arc, or semi section, and is thus expressed,

$$\sqrt{\frac{M^2 + M^2}{2}} \times 3,1416 = \text{arc}, -\tfrac{1}{2}$$

But perhaps the common auger affords the best illustration of these principles, as it embraces both the spiral and elliptical curves, and forever settles the question, in relation to both theories, showing the

---

*) The letters in these Algebraic expressions refer thus: *H* for *hypothenuse* *B* for *base*, and *P* for *perpendicular* also, *M* for *major* and *M* for *minor axis* of the ellipse.

utility of each, at a glance. Observe, that from the bottom upward passing around from the bits about half its circumference, it is not regular in ascending, but increases gradually until it obtains a regular ascent. This corresponds exactly to the elliptical curve. But after it has attained (by constantly increasing its inclination) to regularity, it is then what is termed the spiral line. This shows, that any part of a rail may be obtained (in order to form an easment on a landing), out of the least possible quantity of stuff in thickness, by describing a similar curve to that exhibited by turning an auger upside down, or the bits upward, which are elliptical, and correspond to Plate 14, also, the absurdity of useing that kind of a curve for a continuous flight.

PLATE 21.

Exhibits the method of getting a falling mould by dividing the circle into any number of parts and pointing them off on a line parallel to its base or axis. By this method the pitch of a wall string may be found as the one on Plate 17.

PLATE 22.

Exhibits a plan for a stair the well hole being the frustrum of a cone.

Plate 22.

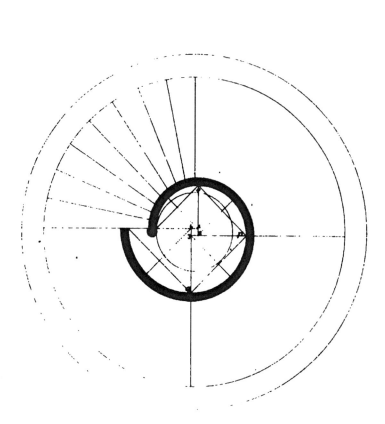

Scale ⅛ in. to 1 foot.

Plate 23.

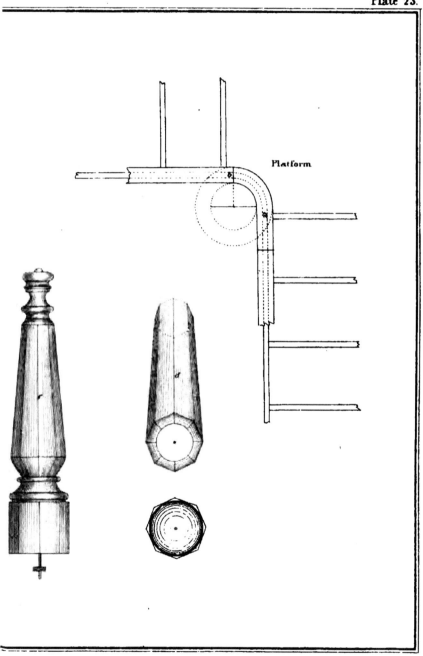

Platform

61

Let the small square in the centre of the diagram, 1, 2, 3, 4, represent the increasing width of the circle as it passes upward, determine the size desired, and set the compass at 1, make the circle to *o*, move the point to 2, and thus pass round to 4, when the inside of the string or handrail as the case may be is completed. It will be seen that each part corresponds to one quarter of the circle, therefore proceed in getting the rail just as in Plate 13 for each quarter circle, adding the correct height to be overcome in the same.

The wall string may be found also as usual, and either glued or keyed up to the wall properly.

PLATE 23.

Exhibits a platform stair the steps running at right angles from the platform.

In laying off this kind, the well hole or face string should be so arranged as to be equal to one of the treads, then it would require no easment in the string and very little in the rail. The rail for these kind of stairs must be got out as on Plate 13 or at least by that principle, as it will be the segment of a larger circle.

c, d, shows a newel post made in the same way as on Plate 10

PLATE 24.

Shows the method of fastening the rail and cap, of an ogee hand rail. Fig. *A* is a top view, the circle at *b* is the hole turned in the cap to hide the bolt head, and *a*, the circle of the ornament to cover it, see Plates 10 and 23.

Fig. *B* shows the bottom, the dotted bolt securing the rail and cap thogether.

The rail should not be worked at the easment until the cap is fitted on it, when it may be dressed to suit it exactly as it makes a much neater job than to work it before hand.

PLATE 25.

This plate shows the method of making the rail pass nearly an equal height from the progressive and retrogressive steps, although the steps may have been wrongly placed in the platform.

Plate 24.

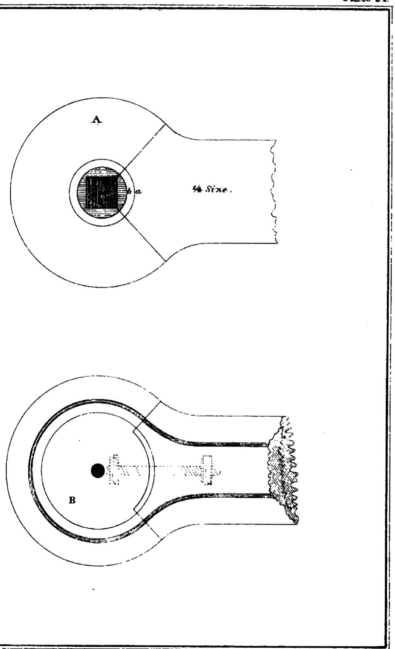

A

½ Size.

B

Plate 25.

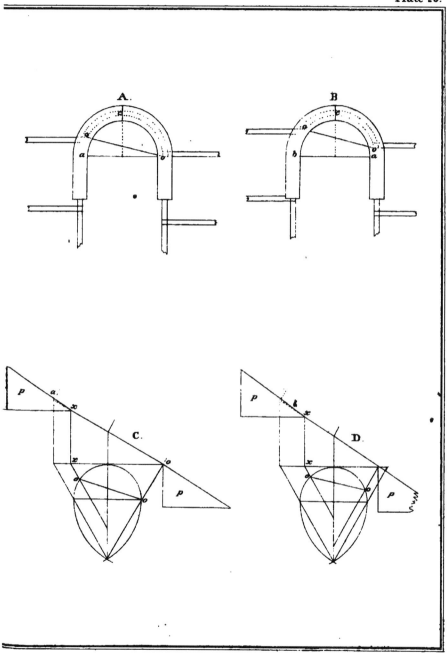

A.

B.

C.

D.

63

Let Fig. *A* be an example, the face of one riser on the axis line of the circle, and the other 3 or 4 inches from the other side, when it is évident, if the rail is worked out in the regular way the balusters must be shorter on the retrogressive flight.

The method of finding the line of the rail in such a case, is shown on Fig. *C*, which is the mould for Fig. *A*. Fig. *B* and *D* are found in the same way.

Take the outstretch of the circle, the exact inside line of the rail, then make the pitch boards correspond to the height of the rail from *o*, passing round to *a*, in the platform *A*. Draw the lines in each case on the outstretch circle the same as in the plan, and erect perpendiculars from the outstretch line, as x, x, to cut the chord line, this gives the angles from which to make the easment and the top line of the rail.

Now as the rail must twist more and raise faster from *c* to *o* on the left than from *o* to *c*, coming up on the right hand side, the moulds for the face of the rail must be got out as on Plates 8 and 11, as the left hand one requires to be an elliptical piece and the right hand one spiral. The spiral piece should be worked from both ends with the bevel taken from the dia-

gram, and the elliptical piece worked as laid down
and described on Plate 8.

The propriety of this method will be seen at once,
as by it, the balusters will be of their proper length,
or nearly so, and will overcome a difficulty very often
experienced by incompetent workmen.

PLATE 26.

Fig. *A* exhibits an elliptical well hole and the
method of obtaining the face mould for the rail by
ordinates, which is the best way of getting it. Lay off
the square 1, 2, 3, 4 cutting the ellipse into four parts,
making a chord line for each, at right angles from
which make the plumb lines 1, 2, 3, 4, 5, 6, &c. &c.
Make the parallel line *a*, and space up the last plumb line
the number of steps as 1, 2, 3, 4, 5, 6, 7, 8, 9, 10,
draw the hypothenuse line, and at right angles, make
the distances from the chord line in the plan, draw
through these points for the inside line of the rail, and
proceed with each piece in the same manner. Let *o*,
in the plan, represent the width of the rail, and plumb
up in the manner here shown or guage from the inside. The bevel to work the twist must be taken from
the pitch board or the hypothenuse line on the diagram. This face mould may be found also by applying
Problem *C*, Plate *B*.

Plate 26.

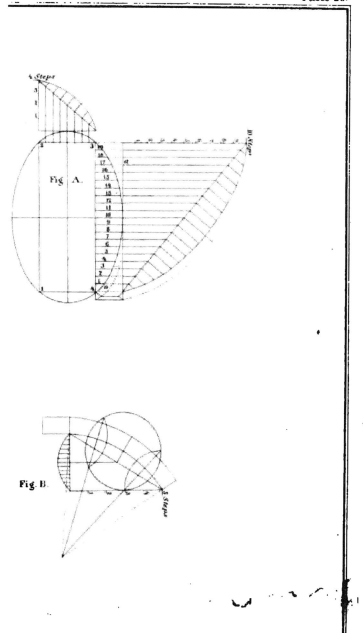

Fig. A.

Fig. B.

65

Fig. *B* exhibits a segment of a larger circle and is the same as on Plate 13, Fig. *A*. Showing 5 steps in height to be overcome in the quarter circle, the plumb lines below show that all the other distances might be taken as the one in the centre, and that they are at right angles to the chord line.

This is if any thing easier than the foregoing methods, the principle however being precisely the same.

INDEX.

Introduction . . . . Pages 3— 6
Explanation of Technical terms . . . . " 7—10
Geometrical Problems . . . . " 11
Sections of a cylinder . . . . " 13
How to make well tubs . . . . " 19—50
How to work rail pieces . . . . " 24—57
How to make falling moulds . . . . " 25—43
How to bore hand rails . . . . " 27
How to make newel posts . . . . " 28
How to find the face moulds for spiral rails . . . . " 31—34
Remarks on the spiral and elliptical lines . . . . . " 39
How to describe one fourth of an ellipse . . . . . " 41
How to construct spiral stair carriages . . . . . . " 45
How to make wall strings . . . . " 47
How to cut down wall strings . . . . " 49
Reasons for adopting these methods . . . . . . " 52
Mathematical demonstrations . . . . " 58—59
How to put on a rail where the steps are wrongly placed
     in the platform . . . . . , ... " 62—64

CPSIA information can be obtained at www.ICGtesting.com
Printed in the USA
LVOW11s2310140913

352492LV00009B/358/P